The ultimate business skills collection
from Bloomsbury Business

The new *Business Essentials* ser
pocket guides on a wide range
performing well in interviews, t
finding the right work/life balan
managing projects effectivel

T0001891

Available from all good retailers and bookshops,
as well as from bloomsbury.com/businessessentials

BLOOMSBURY BUSINESS

Using Social Media for Work

How to maintain professional etiquette online

BLOOMSBURY BUSINESS

LONDON · OXFORD · NEW YORK · NEW DELHI · SYDNEY

BLOOMSBURY BUSINESS
Bloomsbury Publishing Plc
50 Bedford Square, London, WC1B 3DP, UK
29 Earlsfort Terrace, Dublin 2, Ireland

BLOOMSBURY, BLOOMSBURY BUSINESS and the Diana logo are trademarks
of Bloomsbury Publishing Plc

First published in Great Britain in 2023 by Bloomsbury Publishing Plc

A catalogue record for this book is available from the British Library

Library of Congress Cataloguing-in-Publication data has been applied for

ISBN: 978-1-3994-1045-8; eBook: 978-1-3994-1044-1

2 4 6 8 10 9 7 5 3 1

Text design by seagulls.net

Typeset by Deanta Global Publishing Services, Chennai, India
Printed and bound in Great Britain by CPI Group (UK) Ltd, Croydon CR0 4YY

MIX
Paper | Supporting
responsible forestry
FSC® C171272

To find out more about our authors and books visit www.bloomsbury.com
and sign up for our newsletters

Contents

Assess yourself: Are you and your business ready to get results from social media?

Review the following questions and give yourself a score on a scale of one to ten (one being the lowest, ten being the highest).

1. How clearly have you identified your social media goals?
2. Have you identified your target audience and created customer personas?
3. Do you have an active presence on the social media platforms that your target audience uses the most?
4. Have you tailored the information on your social media accounts towards helping your target audience understand how you can help them?

5. Do you have a content calendar?
6. Have you set out a posting schedule?
7. Have you researched the most effective hashtags to use in your social media posts?
8. Do you have a budget for social media advertising?
9. Do you know how to track your performance on social media and measure success?
10. Is your website ready to convert visitors who arrive via social media?

After you have written down your scores, go through the questions again and write down what you would like your ideal score to be.

If you would like your current scores to be higher, aim to write an action plan as you read this book.

Note: At the time of going to print, Twitter has announced a rebrand to X. We refer to the platform as 'X (formerly Twitter)' in this book, but as the terminology of Twitter, Tweet, ReTweet etc is well-known and understood, we have not changed these in the following text. We hope you will be able to swap out the relevant words if required.

1
Getting started with social media

With over 4.76 billion active social media users worldwide (just under 60 per cent of the total global population) and continuing year-on-year growth, it's clear that social media is not just a passing trend.

Getting involved with social media is a valuable way for businesses to increase brand awareness, drive website traffic, generate sales, build customer loyalty, and more.

To get started, we need to understand the social media options that are available to us, clarify what we want to achieve for our business, and ensure that we understand our target audiences.

The world's most-used social media platforms

Let's start by looking at the most used social media platforms, to understand what the best options for you and your business might be.

Social media has become an extremely broad term, characterized by a diverse range of platforms that all, in some way, facilitate social interaction, content creation and sharing. While there is diversity in terms of features and user profiles, there is also a great deal of commonality to be found. The key to success is choosing the most relevant platforms for you and your business, and focusing on getting results from perhaps two or three that are the best fit, rather than trying to spread your resources too thinly across more platforms.

If we rank social media platforms at a global level by monthly active users, Facebook comes out on top with almost 3 billion monthly active users. It's closely followed by YouTube with 2.5 billion monthly active users and Instagram with 2 billion monthly active users (user numbers are as of January 2023).

TikTok, the short-video format platform, became a welcome source of entertainment during the COVID-19 pandemic lockdowns and as a result, the app saw a huge surge in user numbers. It was the most downloaded app in both 2020 and 2021 and tops the user-time chart with Android app users spending an average of 23.5 hours per month on the platform. TikTok is closely followed by another video-focused platform, YouTube, at 23.15 hours use per month. Comparative figures for Facebook are 19.7 hours, Instagram at 12 hours and X (formerly Twitter) at 5.5 hours.

As this book is about using social media for work, you might be surprised that LinkedIn has not yet been mentioned. Owned by Microsoft, LinkedIn's figures are reported differently from other platforms. The best estimate available for comparison is 300 million active monthly users, which places it in the rankings below Snapchat (635 million), Weibo (584 million), X (formerly Twitter) (556 million) and Pinterest (445 million).

However, the data presented above only tells part of the story. For starters, it's global. Yet in every country across the world, there will be different usage patterns. Some platforms, such as Weibo – also known as 微信 – or Weixin have a regional user base (these platforms are both dominant in China), while some countries do not even permit the use of some platforms.

TOP TIP

www.datareportal.com is the recommended resource for platform-by-platform and country-by-country social media data and insights. The information is updated annually and is freely available.

It is important to note that large user numbers do not necessarily mean you have to be present on those social media platforms; other considerations include your business goals, the profile of your target audience and the content you can create for your business. For example, if you are unable to produce video content, TikTok is likely to be unsuitable for you. We will learn more about content for social media in Chapter 4.

Setting goals for using social media

Before diving into setting up your presence on social media platforms, you must be clear on the goals for using social media. If you do not work out your purpose for social media, you can waste a huge amount of time.

Social media is an important place to be, and many benefits can be enjoyed by having a presence and engaging with others.

With a fully optimized profile on your chosen platforms, you will be able to help your business get found by those who might wish to buy from you. Social media is increasingly used as a search tool; in younger demographic groups, it's even taking over as the preferred search engine for online research.

Awareness is the first point of discovery and is key to helping people get to know your business, your products and/or services and your people. After discovery, you will need to stay visible so that your potential customers can learn more about you, build their trust in you and eventually make a purchase. Social media is a valuable tool for supporting awareness goals.

If you have an online presence for your business, perhaps as a showcase for your products and services, or perhaps you are even selling online, social media can be used to drive people to visit your website. This is a simple exercise that involves sharing social media posts about your business and including links to a relevant website page. But do make sure that your website page is ready for visitors and includes all the information a potential customer might need. Surprisingly, many business websites are not designed with a full sales journey in mind and miss out on important information that a potential customer might be looking for, such as an enquiry form or telephone number.

Social media can help a business generate leads by directly engaging with audiences both through content and through comments (on social media posts) and private direct messages. By being active on social media, businesses can build trust and establish relationships that eventually lead to sales.

Although business-to-business and business-to-consumer sales are different – for many reasons – social media can be used by all types of businesses to find customers and generate sales. In addition, social media allows businesses to pay to advertise their products and services. We'll learn more about this in Chapter 5.

Social media is also used to support customers after they have purchased. This could be by efficiently responding to a customer service query sent by direct message, or by building a community around a product or service that will enhance loyalty by bringing people together. Do a search on Facebook for a group about an interest you have – you will likely find a community talking about products that are relevant to its members.

BUSINESS ESSENTIALS

There are also examples of customers sharing their purchases and favourite products on social media – with testimonials, photos and videos. A business should try to engage with any mentions of their products/services online, to show how much you care about your customers and appreciate them investing in and trusting you. Loyal customers will help you build a positive brand reputation and recommend you to their friends, family and colleagues (in turn, leading to more sales).

TOP TIP

Get SMART

Common goals for social media include:

increasing brand awareness;

driving website traffic;

generating leads and sales;

building customer loyalty and advocacy.

Whatever goals you set, make sure they are SMART. That's Specific, Measurable, Achievable, Realistic and Time-related.

By including these five criteria you will be able to maintain focus and track your success.

Here's an example:

XYZ Ltd will use social media to grow its business by an additional 10 per cent revenue over the next 12 months.

We will do this by using Facebook and Instagram to generate awareness about our full range of products, sharing photos and driving traffic to product pages on our website. On the website, we will capture email addresses so that we can send out details of our special offers throughout the year. We will track clicks from website links used in social media posts, and within our email marketing software tag the details of people who have signed up to the mailing list so we can monitor sales that are driven by this activity.

This goal will contribute to the overall business growth strategy and is achievable within the existing resources we have available.

Understanding your target audience on social media

In today's crowded marketplace, businesses that prioritize their customers are more likely to stand out from their competitors and thrive.

Take a moment to think about how well you understand your customers. If your business is well-established, can you describe the characteristics of your best customers? If your business is in a start-up phase, do you have a clear picture of who is most likely to buy from you?

Focusing on the people whom you most want to buy your products or services is essential to success. We call them your target audience, and we can build our understanding of them by creating a customer persona.

A customer persona is a detailed description of your ideal customer; it will include their demographics and their interests. To gather the information, you will need to do some research – talk to people via interviews and surveys – and look for commonalities in their behaviours. Once you have a good understanding of your target audience, research what social media platforms they are using and how they are using them.

Different social media platforms attract different user demographics. For example, Snapchat and TikTok are particularly popular among younger audiences. If you're targeting business professionals, LinkedIn will be a better match. It's far easier to use the same platforms as your target audience, to meet them where they already are, rather than trying to attract them to use a platform that is new and unfamiliar to them.

Cross-reference the details you gather during your customer persona research, with published information, such as that from www.datareportal .com (see page 12) to help you select the best fit for your business to reach your target audience and achieve its business goals.

COMMON MISTAKES

✗ Diving straight in

To get started with social media for work you need to do some planning. It can be too easy to dive into using social media, particularly as it is quick and free to set up an account.

X Trying to do too much

You do not need to use every social media
platform available. You will not have the time
or resources to manage all of them properly.
As part of the planning process, research
the options available and pick two or three
platforms as your primary focus.

BUSINESS ESSENTIALS

✓ Your choice of social media platform should
   not be based on personal experience and
   preferences; for work, you need to have a
   presence on the social media platform/s
   most relevant to helping you achieve your
   business goals, and where you are most likely
   to find your target audience.

✓ For your business to thrive you need to put
   your customers at the heart of your business.
   Carry out some research to understand
   your target audience and create a customer
   persona for your ideal customer.

2
Optimizing your social media profiles

All too often social media profiles are set up quickly; seen as a task to be completed before starting to scroll through the newsfeeds and posting content.

Optimizing your social media profiles means making sure they are set up correctly and in a way that maximizes their potential to help you get found (when people are searching for your business, your products or services, or someone with your specific expertise).

A well-optimized social media profile will also help you improve your credibility and, in turn, build trust with your target audience.

TOP TIP

Your social media profiles should be written with your target audience in mind. You can use your customer personas to tailor language so that it will resonate with them and their needs. Try not to talk too much about yourself; show that you understand your customers and let people know how you can be of help to them.

Step 1: Your profile picture

Your profile picture is one of the first things people will see when they are looking at search results pages or visiting your profile. You only get one chance to make a good first impression, so take time to select a professional photo. If you were to meet up in real life, would your social media profile photo enable someone to recognize you in an office reception, coffee shop or networking event? Ideally, your profile picture will be a professional headshot, where you are looking at the camera (making eye contact with the viewer).

If your social media account is focused on your business, you should use your company logo as your profile photo. Ensure that this fits into the space available for profile photos; some organizations need to create a different version of their logo that fits within a circle or square.

Step 2: Choosing a header image

Some social media platforms – including LinkedIn, X (formerly Twitter) and Facebook – require a header image in addition to a profile picture. This is a great opportunity to brand your profile and use an image that reflects you or your business. It could be a photograph or perhaps a graphic that you create.

Branding your social media profiles helps them to be immediately recognizable, and build credibility and trust. Try to ensure that your branding is consistent across all the social media platforms you are using.

Step 3: About description/bio

Whatever social media platforms you have chosen to use, you will be required to add an about description, or 'bio'. This can vary in character limit across different platforms, so you will need to write this part of your profile carefully.

The about description/bio is a key element of searching on social media, so the words you include will contribute to helping people find you. This means you should try to include the keywords that people might use if they were searching for a business or industry expert like you.

The about description/bio is also displayed in search results, alongside your profile photo, which means it's an important part of making that good first impression.

Step 4: Links to further information

When setting up your social media profiles, there will be options available to include links to further information. Usually, this is one or more website links, so think about what would be most relevant to those viewing your social media profiles. Align the links you use with your business goals, to drive traffic to relevant pages of your website.

As part of the further information you include, double-check that you provide your contact information – an email address and/or telephone number so it's easy for people to get in touch with you.

Step 5: Social proof

To maximize the work-related opportunities social media can bring, it's important to provide

information about your business, products
or services, and personal expertise. Potential
customers will also be looking for social proof
(evidence) in the form of recommendations and
testimonials. Positive reviews can support the
decision-making of existing customers, who may be
evaluating you and your business and comparing
them with competitors.

TOP TIP

Look around at the social media profiles
of other businesses and business profiles.
It can be especially useful to review what
your competitors are doing (and not doing).
Consider what keywords they use, plus what
other information is presented, to stimulate
ideas for the information that you could include
on your profiles.

Step 6: Think about the type of account you want

Where a social media platform has an option to
switch to a professional account, such as Instagram
and TikTok, you will find that this provides access to
more detailed data and insights and that it is highly
worth considering the change.

Some social media platforms, such as LinkedIn and X (formerly Twitter), charge a subscription fee for an account 'upgrade', which will provide users with a range of different features.

Account types and features are subject to regular change; to find out what's currently available, we suggest visiting each social media platform as they will present the options available. As changes are made to the platforms you are using, you will likely receive information as a notification or pop-up.

In the 'where to find more help' section at the end of this book you will find some resources to help you stay on top of social media changes.

Step 7: Settings and privacy

Each social media platform has privacy settings that allow you to stay in control of the information you are sharing online. As a default, these settings tend to be open to all, so it's a good idea to go through the settings to ensure you are fully aware of what can and cannot be seen on your profiles and how other social media users might be able to engage with you.

For example, on Facebook, you can choose who can post on your Page, choose whether you wish to review posts that you're tagged in before the post appears and decide whether you wish to allow people and Pages to send you messages.

On LinkedIn, for example, you can also choose whether to show another user whether you have viewed their profile. You can view profiles anonymously without them being aware – which can sometimes be useful, for example if you are carrying out competitor research or job hunting. Generally, it is better to browse in regular mode so that other users can see your activity and potentially reach out to you, but it's useful to know the private browsing option is also available.

COMMON MISTAKES

✗ Poor profile photos

When you are using social media for work, it's important to present yourself in the most professional way possible. Include a photo, and ensure that it has been taken specifically for your social media account. Do not use photos taken on holiday, for example, or zoom in on yourself as part of a group shot. Consider how you would present yourself in an interview and make a great first impression. Show that you take your business seriously.

✗ Incomplete information

LinkedIn reports that only 51 per cent of users complete all the available sections of information on a profile. By including as much information as possible, you will help people find you and learn as much as they can about you.

BUSINESS ESSENTIALS

✓ Take time to optimize your social media profiles. Research what each of your chosen platforms requires and ensure that you complete all the sections available.

✓ Focus on writing your social media profile to appeal to your target audience. Use keywords to help them find you during an online search and to resonate with their interests when they read more details.

✓ Re-visit your social media profiles regularly (perhaps every three months) to ensure that they are up to date and incorporate any feature changes that might have been added.

3
Managing your social media accounts like a pro

There's no doubt that, even once everything has been set up, social media can be very time-consuming to manage.

Social media requires being social – you need to spend time with your followers and connections. You need to post content that's of interest to them and you need to respond to the content they are posting; all in a timely manner.

Step 1: Set up notifications

In the previous chapter, we advised you to check through the privacy and settings on each social media platform. Here, you will also find options for receiving notifications. Deciding what you do and do not wish to be alerted about is a great way to help you manage your social media accounts.

For example, on Instagram, you can receive a notification when someone likes or comments on a post, when someone mentions you in a post or comment, or when someone starts following you.

It can be useful to receive notifications when you are mentioned in a post, as it allows you to monitor what is being said and to respond to any comments promptly.

Step 2: Focus on consistency

Consistency is key when it comes to managing social media, and building a regular habit of content creation, posting, building your followers and engaging with your community is far easier (in the long term) than ad hoc batches of time. Your followers will also appreciate consistency as they will regularly be able to see you in their newsfeeds. You never know when the time will be right to win business from your followers, so a front-of-mind positioning at all times will help you achieve success on social media.

Consistent activity will help you build awareness and establish credibility and trust. Your followers will become familiar with your business, your expertise and your products or services. As social media moves fast, not all your content will be seen by your followers – the more consistently you show up, the greater the chances of your followers recognizing you, and paying attention.

Social media platforms also value consistent activity. Each platform is built on a set of rules and calculations that helps prioritize what its users see in their newsfeed. We call these rules and calculations algorithms. They change often and are different for each platform.

While many 'myths' are shared about what social media algorithms prioritize, we can be confident that they all focus on increasing use and engagement on their platform, and therefore prioritize showing its users content that they will find most relevant, based on their known behaviour, interests and interactions on the platform.

Step 3: Schedule your posts

Although social media happens in real time, it's useful to know that you can manage your own time by scheduling posts in advance.

Most social media platforms, including Facebook, Instagram, X (formerly Twitter), LinkedIn, TikTok and Weibo, allow users to schedule posts to be released at a pre-defined time and date. This can be particularly useful if you operate in a different time zone to your customers. It can also be useful if you are preparing a batch of posts and wish to schedule them in one go – for example, if you are involved with an event, you might wish to prepare a series of social media posts and have them ready to go out over a period of time.

It is important to note, however, that the social element of social media means that you cannot just 'set and forget' your posts; you should be available to respond to any comments.

Step 4: Prioritize engagement

Engagement on social media refers to the interactions and actions that users take in response to your content. This can include likes, comments, shares and clicks.

When your followers engage with your content, it indicates that they find it interesting and valuable. You can take this opportunity to continue the conversation – say thank you, add further

BUSINESS ESSENTIALS

comments and, if you can, aim to book a meeting to discuss the content further.

You should also prioritize engaging with the content your followers post – that becomes visible in your newsfeeds. Look out for your target audience posting content that you can get involved with, by adding a like or a comment.

By engaging with your followers, you can build stronger relationships, credibility and trust – key ingredients for successful customer acquisition and retention.

TOP TIP

Responding to comments and messages on social media is important; not only do you not want to be seen as ignoring your followers and missing out on potential opportunities, but it's a great way to enhance your reputation and build and maintain relationships.

✓ Be timely: respond to comments and messages as soon as possible to show your audience that you value them. Research shows that social media users expect a reply to public or private messages within three hours.

✓ Be professional: always respond courteously, even if you receive negative feedback or criticism. This can help mitigate the damage to your reputation and might enhance customer loyalty and advocacy if the contact is seen to have been well managed.

Step 5: Use social media management tools

If you are managing multiple social media accounts, you might find it useful to use a separate management tool that centralizes access to your newsfeeds, allows scheduling, monitoring of mentions and more. Most tools have a trial version available, and different levels of paid-for options based on the number of profiles added, features and user numbers.

Here are a few suggested tools:

Buffer

Buffer is a popular social media management tool that helps you schedule posts across multiple social media platforms and profiles. Visit www.buffer.com for more information.

Hootsuite

Hootsuite is another popular social media management tool that allows you to manage multiple social media profiles from a single dashboard. It supports platforms including X (formerly Twitter), Facebook, Instagram, LinkedIn, Pinterest, YouTube and TikTok. Hootsuite also has an online learning academy and free certification to learn more about social media and social media management. Visit www.hootsuite.com for more information.

MeetEdgar

MeetEdgar is a social media scheduling tool that allows you to organize, recycle and reuse content, making it easy to keep your account active. Visit www.meetedgar.com for more information.

Sprout Social

Sprout Social is a social media management and intelligence tool, used by over 30,000 brands around the world for scheduling content across multiple platforms, delivering customer service, as well as social media listening and employee advocacy. Visit www.sproutsocial.com for more information.

Step 6: Consider outsourcing

If you have limited knowledge and resources within your business, you might consider hiring a marketing expert to help you with your social media planning and day-to-day management. They could help take away some of the content creation, posting and inbox management work for you.

Some useful platforms for finding freelancers include Fiverr, Upwork, PeoplePerHour and LinkedIn. Find the Services Marketplace on LinkedIn and search for 'social media marketing'.

BUSINESS ESSENTIALS

COMMON MISTAKES

✗ Getting distracted

Social media can take you down a rabbit hole of scrolling through newsfeeds, looking at images and watching videos. Keep your goals in mind at all times and stay focused on what you are looking to achieve when using social media.

✗ Forgetting to be 'social'

So much time can be spent on creating and posting that social media users can forget to be social and engage with others. This can lead to missing opportunities for meaningful connections, building credibility and trust.

BUSINESS ESSENTIALS

✔ Build your social media management toolkit

Time management is essential in business, so take a look at what resources you already have and seek out tools that can support your productivity. This includes possible outsourcing of work and the use of scheduling tools.

✔ Create a habit

To build your social media presence, you will need to be consistent on social media by posting content regularly and being visible in your followers' newsfeeds. Creating a habit of scheduling and planning social media activity will help you do this and achieve the results you're looking for.

4
Where to find ideas for social media content

Constantly coming up with fresh ideas for social media can be a challenging task. Fortunately, there are plenty of ways to find inspiration, from asking your customers what they want to see to getting involved with trending topics.

It's a good idea to create a content calendar, setting out in advance what you will be posting on your chosen platforms, and when.

An ideal mix of content in your plan would be to follow the social media 'rule of thirds':

1. One-third of your content should be about promoting yourself and your business.
2. One-third of your content should be recommending interesting stuff: 'how to' articles, industry research, latest trends etc.

3. One-third of your content should let your audience get to know you better: share interesting things about what you're doing behind the scenes of your business.

'How often should I post?' is a common question asked in relation to using social media for work. In the previous chapter, we noted the importance of consistency. We also highlighted the resources you might have available in-house and whether you might consider outsourcing some parts of your social media planning and management. These factors will drive part of the answer to the question. Another important factor is relevance – you should post when you have something interesting and relevant for your target audience; social media should not be about posting for the sake of posting. This will not help you achieve engagement or, ultimately, your business goals.

BUSINESS ESSENTIALS

TOP TIP

For most social media platforms, including Facebook and LinkedIn, posting content once per day or a few times per week can be a good starting point.

On visual platforms, such as Instagram and TikTok, posting more frequently, such as once or twice a day, may be more effective.

You will need to experiment with different posting frequencies and times to find the optimal schedule for your specific audience and business goals.

Content types

Content is the foundation of your social media presence; it's how you build and maintain a relationship with your customers.

With billions of people actively using social media every day, it's more important than ever to create high-quality, engaging content that stands out from the competition. It's important to know your audience and tailor your content to their preferences and interests.

Each social media platform has its own requirements, from character limits to image sizes and video specifications. Using the wrong format will result in content being cut off, distorted or pixelated. It's a good idea to search for the latest details for each platform and ensure you prepare your content in the most appropriate way.

Make sure it is easy to read and that you include clear calls to action so that your followers know what to do after viewing your post. Do you want them to answer a question, register for an event or visit a website page for example?

There are four types of content to consider for social media:

1. Written content
2. Visual content
3. Audio content
4. Video content

All platforms need written content, whether that's the main format of the post, or text to support an image or video. Text is searchable across social media, so needs to include the keywords about your business, area of expertise, products and services to help you get found.

Visual content such as photos and graphics can be a powerful tool for businesses to use to attract the attention of their audience. Instagram, Pinterest and TikTok are particularly well suited for visual content.

TOP TIP

If you can source your own photography, this will be unique to your business and more engaging for your audience. However, if your resources are limited, you can source imagery from online libraries such as www.unsplash.com, www.pixabay.com and www.shutterstock.com

A popular tool to support creating professional designs, without the need for graphic design expertise, is Canva (www.canva.com). Canva provides a user-friendly drag-and-drop design tool, plus many templates and images to help you create social media posts.

Currently, the most engaging content format for social media is video. YouTube, TikTok and Reels on Facebook and Instagram provide the opportunity to share a video that captures attention, provides information and can also be entertaining. There are many options available for creating video content for social media, including live streaming, short-form videos (less than three minutes) and long-form videos (more than three minutes).

TOP TIP

When planning video content:

✓ Focus on the first three seconds of the video so that you capture the attention of your viewers quickly.

✓ Make sure the sound quality is good. You may need to use an external microphone if you're using a smartphone.

✓ Aim for natural lighting.

✓ If you use music, make sure you do not breach copyright laws.

✓ End with a call-to-action; what would you like your viewers to do next?

Some social media platforms provide a unique opportunity for ephemeral content, that is content that is only available for a limited time. Examples include Instagram Stories and Snapchat Snaps. They are only available for 24 hours and have become popular for producing authentic behind-the-scenes content, promoting time-limited offers and providing live event coverage.

Audio content has become increasingly popular, with platforms like Clubhouse and features such as Twitter Spaces and LinkedIn Audio events introducing new ways for users to share and consume content in a sound-only format. Audio content can also be more convenient for users who prefer to consume content while multitasking or on the go, as it doesn't require the same level of visual attention as other content formats. Social media posts are also great for sharing podcast content.

Content to address customer pain points

Use the information in your customer personas to guide you to create content that will resonate with your target audience. Pain points are the specific problems, challenges or frustrations that your customers experience and addressing these as part of your content will help you build awareness and relationships with your followers.

They will see how much you understand them and are the right people to help them.

Here's some examples:

- create a how-to video that addresses a pain point;

- create a series of images that provide top tips for overcoming a common problem;

- share success stories provided by customers who have worked with you to overcome similar challenges.

Content that goes behind the scenes of your business

When it comes to social media content, one idea that can help businesses stand out and build a strong connection with their followers is sharing behind-the-scenes glimpses of their business.

Whether it's showcasing the production process, introducing team members or sharing sneak peeks of upcoming projects, behind-the-scenes content can help humanize your brand and foster a sense of authenticity and connection.

- A restaurant or other food outlet could share photos or videos of their chefs preparing meals, giving followers an inside look at how their favourite dishes are made.

- A clothing brand could show its full design process, from sketching to fabric selection to the finished product.

✓ A tech start-up could share photos or videos of
   their team working on new features, providing
   insight into the development process.

Sharing behind-the-scenes content can also help
businesses build excitement and anticipation for
upcoming launches or events.

Content for key dates

We're conditioned to celebrate key dates
throughout the year, from birthdays to anniversaries
and public holidays. You will also have key dates
and milestones within your business that can be a
source of social media content. Look through your
calendar and make a note of occasions you could
celebrate; think about your business, your products,
your employees etc. Also consider events such as
reaching a specific number of learners for an online
training course, or achieving a record level of users
for your product.

As well as public holidays, there are a wide variety
of awareness days and events throughout the
year, covering topics such as health and wellness,
environmental issues and more. You can create
content to align with awareness days if you can
link the topic to your business activities in a
meaningful way.

Here are some popular awareness days:

International Women's Day – 8 March

International Women's Day is a global event that celebrates women's achievements and raises awareness of gender inequality.

Earth Day – 22 April

Earth Day is an annual event that aims to promote environmental awareness and encourage people to take action to protect the planet.

Pride Month – June

LGBTQ+ Pride Month is dedicated to the celebration of lesbian, gay, bisexual and transgender pride.

World Mental Health Day – 10 October

This day aims to raise awareness about mental health issues around the world and promote positive mental health practices.

International Volunteer Day – 5 December

This is a day to recognize and promote volunteers and community service.

TOP TIP

Plan out the key dates you might create social media content for and add them to your content calendar.

Here are some useful resources:

- www.onthisday.com lists historical events for history, film, music and sport plus birthdays for important and famous people;

- www.timeanddate.com/holidays share holidays and observances around the world;

- www.daysoftheyear.com lists national and international holidays plus awareness days.

Trending topics

A trending topic on social media is a subject, issue, event or conversation that is being widely discussed on social media, at a point in time. It is characterized by a high volume of mentions or engagement related to a particular topic or keyword (hashtag).

Using trending topics as content for social media is a great way for businesses to tap into an existing buzz and increase their own visibility. You will need to make quick decisions to get involved with trending topics because they can disappear quickly (when the next news item comes along).

Finding out what's trending can be done in a few ways, depending on the platform you are using:

● X (formerly Twitter):

On X, you can see what's trending in the 'What's happening' section on the right-hand side of your desktop newsfeed.

● LinkedIn:

On LinkedIn, you can see a 'News' section on the right-hand side of your desktop homepage. You can also follow LinkedIn News to receive daily notifications of the latest business, career and economic news in your region.

Visit: https://www.linkedin.com/showcase/linkedin-news/

● TikTok:

On TikTok, you can see what's trending by exploring the 'Discover' section. This section shows you popular videos, sounds and hashtags that are trending on the platform.

● **Weibo:**

On Weibo, you can check out the 'Hot Topics' section to find out what's trending.

TOP TIP

Hashtags

Hashtags are not just for trending topics – they are a useful way to maximize the visibility of your content on social media.

Adding a # symbol in front of a word or phrase as part of your social media post is a good way to help users see what your post is about. There should be no spaces between words and symbols in a hashtag.

Using a hashtag turns the word or phrase into a clickable link – taking people through to more content about the topic. If people are searching social media for a specific topic, this is how they might be able to find you. Consider what words people might be searching for – these are the hashtags to include (there's no need to overthink it).

If you're not sure, there are several tools available that can help you find the right

---

hashtags to use on social media, including Hashtagify, RiteTag and Tagomatic.

Here are some examples of how hashtags are used on different social media platforms. You can observe the latest use and best practices for hashtags by looking at what other users are doing.

X (formerly Twitter): Hashtags were first used on Twitter, so they are highly recommended. However, it's important not to overdo it. Use two to three hashtags per Tweet.

Instagram: You can use up to 30 hashtags per post on Instagram; you might use more when you are starting off with Instagram, and fewer when your account is more established. It's best to focus on highly relevant hashtags to help your posts get found. The more specific you can be, the better. For example, '#love' is very broad, '#lovebooks' is more relevant for those interested in books and reading.

Facebook: While Facebook supports hashtags, they are less commonly used than on X and Instagram. They are used most often in relation to a specific campaign, perhaps a large event such as #LondonMarathon, for example.

User-generated content

User-generated content (UGC) is a powerful way for businesses to engage with their followers on social media. UGC can take many forms, such as product reviews, photos or videos of customers using your products, or stories about how your brand has impacted their lives. Instagram Stories and Reels are particularly well suited for UGC, as they allow businesses to easily re-share and feature customer content.

UGC can happen naturally, or you can offer your followers a little encouragement to create and share content related to your brand. Perhaps run a social media competition on World Photography Day (18 August) with a prize for the best image.

A cosmetics brand could encourage customers to share photos or videos of their make-up looks using the brand's products. A cleaning product manufacturer could encourage customers to share photos or videos of how they use the products in their homes. A coffee shop could ask customers to share photos of their drinks on Instagram. A webinar host could encourage photos of specific slides in their presentation.

Customers generally include a mention of the products they feature in their posts, which makes it easy to spot and share. Suggesting the use of a branded hashtag is also a good idea.

UGC helps businesses increase their reach and brand awareness. When customers share their content related to your brand, it can be seen by their followers, who may not have heard of your business, products or services before. This can help you reach a wider audience and build credibility through free word-of-mouth marketing.

COMMON MISTAKES

✗ No content calendar

A content calendar will also help you stay organized and ensure that your content is varied and balanced.

✗ Trendjacking

It can be useful to get involved with an awareness day or trending topic, but if it's not relevant to your business, the association could backfire and damage your brand reputation. Be sure not to be insensitive or disrespectful by getting involved with a subject currently in the news.

BUSINESS ESSENTIALS

✔ Quality over quantity

It's better to post less often and deliver high-quality, engaging content than to post more frequently with mediocre content.

✔ Test and learn

There's no silver bullet to getting results from social media, and the pace of change is fast. You will need to experiment with different types of content and adjust your content calendar often. Looking at measurements of success will help you to know what is working, and what isn't. We will look at this in Chapter 6.

5
An introduction to social media advertising

The outbreak of COVID-19 accelerated the adoption of social media In turn, brands increased their spending on social media advertising.

Types of social media advertising

Social media platforms provide paid-for options to help businesses to reach greater numbers of people. The options do vary by platform but generally, fall into a few main categories.

1. Pay-per-click (PPC) advertising – this type of advertising charges a business when an ad receives a click. The click could be to a lead generation form, or a page on your website.

2. Display advertising – this involves placing banner ads on a social media platform. Businesses are typically charged based on the number of times the ad is shown (displayed) to a social media user. These ad displays are called 'impressions'.

3. Sponsored content – some platforms, such as LinkedIn, offer businesses the opportunity to pay to have their content appear in users' news feeds.

Transparency around advertising is a legal requirement in many countries; it is also important for building trust with users. Therefore, labels such as 'sponsored' or 'promoted' are used on content so that a user can be aware that they are seeing an advertisement for a product or service.

Each platform has rules around what can and cannot be promoted, along with some restrictions on targeting (for example, on some platforms you cannot advertise to users aged under 18). Restricted products include adult products, alcohol, gaming and medical items. You will find guidelines on the platform websites.

Self-service tools for social media advertising

Setting up social media advertising campaigns has never been easier thanks to the self-serve tools that each platform provides.

Some platforms offer the option to 'boost' a post, which means adding some budget to an organic post on your profile, to extend its reach to more people. Boosted posts are designed to increase the visibility of an organic post to a wider audience, but they do not offer the same level of targeting or customization as social media advertising.

Facebook Ads Manager, LinkedIn Campaign Manager and TikTok Ads Manager are just a few examples of the self-serve tools available to businesses. These platforms provide easy-to-follow steps for creating and launching advertising campaigns, making it accessible to businesses of all sizes and budgets.

The workflow may vary slightly by platform, but the key steps you will be asked to follow are:

Step 1: Choose your objective

The first step for social media advertising is to choose your objective. These are usually displayed under three key headings – awareness, consideration and conversion.

Awareness objectives aim to increase brand awareness and reach a broader audience. The goal is to introduce the brand to potential customers who may not have heard of it before. Examples of awareness objectives include promoting a new product or service, building brand awareness or reaching a new target audience.

Consideration objectives aim to encourage potential customers to engage further with the brand and consider its products or services. Examples of consideration objectives include driving website traffic, generating leads or encouraging app downloads.

Conversion objectives aim to drive specific actions from potential customers, such as making a purchase, signing up for a service or filling out a form. Examples of conversion objectives include driving online sales, promoting a sale or special offer or encouraging in-store visits.

Step 2: Select your audience criteria

At this next step, you need to choose who you want to see your ad. There are various options here, from the people who already follow your page, to selecting specific audience criteria using demographics (age, gender, location) and/or specific interests. You can also select audiences based on previous interactions with your profile or even visitors to your website.

Again, this is where the information collected as part of your customer persona research can be useful. The more you know about your target audience, the more effective your advertising will be.

Step 3: Set your schedule

You can choose to run your ads continuously or only during a specific date range. This could be to coincide with a promotional offer period, or perhaps to tie in with an event you are hosting. Bear in mind that ads tend to start in a 'learning phase' where the delivery system is exploring the best way to deliver your advertisements (including placements and frequency), therefore you might want to factor in a minimum of seven days' running time for your advertisement, especially if you're new to advertising.

TOP TIP

'Automated Placements' is a useful feature within Facebook Ads Manager that allows advertisers to place their ads on multiple Meta platforms, i.e. Facebook, Instagram, WhatsApp and Messenger.

Ads Manager will automatically select the best placements based on the campaigns' objective, budget and target audience, ensuring that the ad is shown in the places it's most likely to perform best.

Step 4: Set your budget

The amount of budget needed to get started with social media advertising varies depending on the platform and the advertising objectives. Some platforms like Facebook and Instagram allow for advertising with as little as $1 a day, while others like LinkedIn may require a higher minimum spend. It's better to start with a smaller budget and gradually increase it as you see positive results and gain more experience with social media advertising.

When setting up a social media advertising campaign, you'll need to decide whether to use a lifetime budget or a daily budget. A lifetime budget is a one-time amount you're willing to spend on a campaign for the duration of its lifetime, while a daily budget is a fixed amount you're willing to spend per day.

Choosing a lifetime budget may be beneficial if you have a specific end date in mind for your campaign or if you want to control the total spend. On the other hand, a daily budget can provide more flexibility in terms of adjusting spending levels on a daily basis and can be a good option if you're testing different ad variations or if you want to maintain a consistent presence over a longer period of time.

Step 5: Create your ad

The format of your ad on social media will depend on your selected objectives. It will also differ by platform. Common options for your ads are:

- image;

- video;

- carousel (multiple images or videos in a single ad).

You have just a few seconds while people are scrolling to capture attention, so use bold imagery in your advertising and include your brand identity early on. As with organic content, each platform will have its own specifications for advertising, so check that you are preparing them correctly to ensure the best results.

Before you go live with your social media advertisement, you will get the option to preview your ads and see how they will look on different devices (desktop, mobile, tablet). Using the Ad Manager tools you will be able to monitor how the ads are working and make any changes you require, at any time.

TOP TIP

If you're looking for examples of social media advertisements, visit Facebook's Ad Library. You will not be able to see audience targeting or budget information, but you will be able to view ads that are currently running on Facebook and Instagram including the text, images and videos used in the ads.

The library was created in response to concerns about political advertising and misinformation on social media platforms and it is intended to increase transparency and accountability around advertising on Facebook. It's fully searchable and available at www.facebook.com/ads/library

On LinkedIn, you can view advertisements by visiting any Company Page. If they are currently running ads then you will be able to view 'posts', which are separated by content type, including ads.

TikTok also has a creative centre where you can view case studies and examples of top-performing ads. Visit www.ads.tiktok.com

COMMON MISTAKES

✗ Poor targeting

One of the biggest mistakes in social media advertising is not targeting the right audience. If the targeting is too broad or too narrow, the ad may not be effective or reach the intended audience. Look carefully at the various interest options available within the self-serve advertising platforms.

✗ Starting with a conversion objective

A common mistake with social media advertising is going straight for a conversion objective without first generating awareness. While it may be tempting to jump straight into driving sales or sign-ups, it's important to remember that users may not be familiar with your brand, product or service. If a user has never heard of your brand, they are unlikely to make a purchase or sign up for a service on their first encounter with your ad.

BUSINESS ESSENTIALS

✓ Include a call-to-action

When you spend money on advertising, you need to generate results for your business. Be clear on the call-to-action you include when setting up your ad campaign.

✓ Testing

It's essential to test different ad formats, targeting criteria and messaging to optimize the ad's performance and increase your return on advertising spend (ROAS).

6
Tracking your social media performance

At the beginning of this book, we suggested setting SMART goals. The M stands for Measurement; so, from the very beginning, you should set out what success would look like for you in using social media.

There's a huge amount of data available via social media platforms, so it's important to work out what you need to know and focus on the information that will let you know how you are doing when compared against your business goals.

Some of the data will be performance data, helping you track performance along the way to your overall goals.

TOP TIP

Look for data that tells you what is performing
well in terms of helping you grow your business
and achieve your goals.

Put simply, do more of what is working and less
of what isn't working so well.

For each of the social media platforms you are
using, the key social media metrics that you should
be monitoring regularly are:

✔ **Follower growth:** Follower growth is a measure
of the rate at which your social media following
is increasing over time. While follower count
alone doesn't necessarily indicate success,
tracking your follower growth can help you
understand how well your social media efforts
are resonating with new audiences and can help
you adjust your content strategy to continue to
attract new followers.

✔ **Reach:** Reach refers to the number of unique
users who have seen your content on social
media. This metric is important because it gives
you an idea of how many people are being
exposed to your brand through your social
media efforts.

Impressions: Impressions refer to the total number of times your content has been seen on social media, regardless of whether it was seen by a unique user or not. This metric can give you a better sense of the overall exposure your content is receiving on social media. However, it's important to note that impressions alone don't necessarily indicate success – it's important to look at other metrics such as engagement and conversion rates to understand the full impact of your social media efforts.

Engagement: Engagement refers to any action taken by users on your social media content, such as likes, comments, shares and clicks. This metric is important because it gives you a sense of how well your content is resonating with your audience. High engagement rates can indicate that your content is relevant, interesting and valuable to your audience. By monitoring engagement, you can adjust your content plan to include more of what's working well and less of what isn't.

Engagement rate: Engagement rate is a measure of the engagement your content is receiving relative to your followers. To calculate your engagement rate, divide your total engagement (likes, comments, shares, clicks) by your followers and multiply by 100. For example, if your post had 100 likes, 10 comments and 5 shares, and you have 1,000 followers, your engagement rate would be ((100+10+5)/1,000) x 100 = 11.5 per cent. Monitoring your engagement rate closely can help you understand the effectiveness of your content in driving engagement and connecting with your audience. It also provides a useful benchmark for comparison across your content.

Click-through rate (CTR): CTR is a measure of the percentage of users who click on your social media content after seeing it. To calculate your CTR, divide the number of clicks your content received by your total impressions and multiply by 100. Monitoring your CTR can help you understand how effective your social media content is at driving traffic to your website or other desired destination.

Conversion rate: Conversion rate is a measure of the percentage of users who take a desired action on your website after clicking through from your social media content. This could include actions like making a purchase, signing up for a newsletter or filling out a contact form.

✓ **Video views:** For video content, each social media platform provides different metric information. A common metric, however, is to count a view when a video has been played for at least three seconds. You can also take a look at view-through rates (VTR), that is how many users watched the whole video from start to end.

In addition to monitoring the organic performance of your social media content, it's important to also measure the performance of any social media advertising. Here are some additional metrics to look at:

✓ **Cost per click (CPC):** CPC is a measure of the average cost you pay for each click on your social media ad. To calculate CPC, divide the total amount spent on your ad campaign by the number of clicks your ad received.

✓ **Return on ad spend (ROAS):** ROAS is a measure of the revenue generated by your social media advertising campaign relative to the amount spent on the campaign. To calculate ROAS, divide the total revenue generated by the campaign by the amount spent on the campaign. For example, if your campaign generated $10,000 in revenue and you spent $1,000 on the campaign, your ROAS would be 10.

✓ **Cost per acquisition (CPA):** CPA is a measure of the average cost you pay for each conversion generated by your social media advertising campaign. To calculate your CPA, divide the total amount spent on the campaign by the number of conversions generated.

Tools for tracking social media performance

Thankfully, there are many tools available to help you track your social media performance. Here are a few of the most popular ones:

1. Native platform insights

Each social media platform will provide its own data and insights. For some platforms, such as Instagram and TikTok, you might need to switch to a professional account to access this.

When you access your account insights you will be able to see details about your content, including reach, impressions and engagement.

For some platforms you will also be able to access useful data about your followers, including age, gender and location. This is a good way to check your social media audience matches your desired audience (as discovered as part of your customer persona research). You will also be able to see when your followers are most likely to be online; this is your indicator of the best times of day to post your content. Consider scheduling posts to go live during the times when your followers are most active to increase your reach and engagement.

2. Social media management tools

Social media management tools, such as Hootsuite, include features that allow you to track your performance across multiple social media platforms. Often, you can tailor your own reporting dashboards within these tools, which can be both valuable and time-saving.

3. Google Analytics

Google Analytics is a comprehensive analytics tool that provides data on your website's performance. It can also be used to track social media performance, providing valuable insights into how your social media efforts are impacting your website.

To specifically track social media traffic in Google Analytics, you'll need to set up tracking parameters called UTM links, or UTMs. By adding UTMs to your social media posts, you will be able to see which social media posts and platforms are driving the most traffic to your website, and the user's behaviour once on the website, e.g. what pages they look at, how long they spend on each page etc. For the most detailed level of insights, you will need to set up separate links for each separate item you want to track. This could be a separate link for each social media post, and also for each social media platform you post on.

Here's an example of how to set up a UTM link for use in a social media post.

Let's say that you're sharing a link to a blog post on X (formerly Twitter). The original link might look something like this:

www.yourwebsite.com/blogpost

To add UTM codes to this link, you would use the Google Analytics Campaign URL Builder. The URL Builder allows you to add parameters to your link that will be tracked in Google Analytics.

Here's how you would set up UTM codes for a Twitter link:

1. Go to the Google Analytics Campaign URL Builder: https://ga-dev-tools.appspot.com/campaign-url-builder/

2. Enter the URL of the page you're linking to in the Website URL field.

3. In the Campaign Source field, enter 'Twitter' or the name of the social media platform you're sharing the link on.

4. In the Campaign Medium field, enter 'social' or 'social media'.

5. In the Campaign Name field, enter a name for the campaign that will help you identify it in Google Analytics.

6. Click 'Generate URL' to create the tagged link.

The tagged link will look something like this:

www.yourwebsite.com/blogpost?utm_source =Twitter&utm_medium=socialmedia&utm_ campaign=BlackFridayPromo

When someone clicks on this link, the UTM link will be tracked in Google Analytics, allowing you to see how much traffic is coming from X (formerly Twitter) and which tweets are driving the most traffic.

Don't worry that this link looks a bit long and messy. If you're using a social media management tool such as Buffer or Hootsuite, you can shorten the link. Some platforms such as LinkedIn will automatically shorten the link natively. Alternatively, you can use an independent tool to create shortened links, for example bit.ly. Instagram does not currently allow links to be included with a post, however, you could use a UTM link within your bio link options.

COMMON MISTAKES

✗ Vanity metrics

Often, businesses will get hooked on metrics that do not match against their business goals. They seek out high numbers of followers and engagements and forget about conversions and sales.

✗ Missing the engagement opportunity

Engagement is the key to social media. Whenever a user engages with your content – a like, comment or share – it displays that action to others, which in turn will help to increase your reach and visibility. In your post, don't forget to let people know what action you want them to take next. Measure your performance against your chosen call-to-action.

BUSINESS ESSENTIALS

✓ Review your social media data and insights monthly. This is best practice and will allow you to track how you are progressing towards your SMART goals.

✓ Focus on the metrics that matter most to your business. Set your own benchmarks for success and look for continual improvement when you are doing your monthly review.

7
Best practices and pitfalls to avoid on social media

Achieving results on social media takes time. Please do not expect to find any 'quick wins' or to become an overnight success; it rarely happens!

To maintain professional etiquette online, there are some recommended best practices. These include:

Being authentic

Authenticity is key when it comes to social media. Your followers want to see the real you, not a carefully curated image. Authenticity will build trust and credibility, and support the development of relationships and business opportunities.

Engaging with your followers

Social media is a two-way conversation. Respond to comments, messages and reviews in a timely and respectful manner. Show your followers that you appreciate their support, and respect and value their feedback.

TOP TIP

Commenting on other users' content on social media is also an important aspect of building relationships. By leaving thoughtful and relevant comments on other users' posts, you are showing that you are interested in what they have to say and that you value their content.

Direct messages (DMs) provide a more personal and private way to communicate with other users, which can help you to establish a deeper connection and foster trust. You can use DMs to reach out to new followers, respond to messages from existing followers and connect with other users in your industry or niche.

Staying up to date with trends and changes

Social media is constantly evolving and it's important to stay up to date with trends and changes. Not only will this show your followers that you understand how social media works, but you will also see better results from your efforts if you understand current best practices and can take advantage of new features.

It is important to be aware of the current news agenda to ensure that your content is empathetic with events. For example, some posts could be considered insensitive during a national tragedy or crisis.

Checking spelling and grammar

Attention to spelling and grammar is important to your professional reputation. It's easy to make a mistake, so try using a tool such as www.grammarly .com to check your work. A free Google Chrome extension is available that works with social media platforms natively, and some social media management tools.

Ensuring your content is accessible

Accessibility means making sure that everyone, regardless of their abilities, can access and view your social media content.

Here are some ways to ensure that your social media posts are accessible:

✓ Use alt text

Alt text is a description of an image that is read by screen readers. Be short and succinct when you are describing the content. There is no need to include 'image of' or 'photo of'. You can include alt text when you post natively or via social media management platforms.

✓ Use captioning

Captioning is the process of adding text to videos. It's not only important to individuals who are deaf or hard of hearing but also benefits those who are in a noisy environment or watching videos without sound. Many social media platforms provide automatic captioning features.

✓ Be careful with emojis

Emojis should enhance your message, not replace it. Avoid using emojis in place of words or phrases, and avoid repeating emojis. When a screen reader is used, the use of emojis can make a social media post more confusing. Also, be aware that emojis can have different meanings in different countries, for example, the 'thumbs up' emoji is commonly used as a positive symbol in Western cultures, but in some Middle Eastern countries, it is considered an offensive gesture.

✓ Use CamelCase for hashtags

When using hashtags in your content, it is best practice to capitalize the first letter of each word to make it clear where the new word begins. For example, #InternationalWomensDay or #BlackLivesMatter.

✓ Use high colour contrast

When creating images, ensure that any colour contrast is high, i.e. there is a significant difference in brightness to allow people to distinguish between different colours. White and yellow, for example, would not be considered high colour contrast.

✓ Consider your images

In particular, do not use flashing images. This is important for people with epilepsy or other neurological conditions.

Pitfalls to avoid

Throughout this book, we have learned about the significant use and opportunity provided by social media. However, with opportunity comes risk and there are some pitfalls to avoid.

Being too self-promotional

One of the biggest mistakes businesses make on social media is being too self-promotional.

Constantly promoting your products or services can turn off your followers and make your social media presence feel like an advertisement. Instead, focus on providing value to your audience through informative or entertaining content. Show, don't tell.

Posting insensitive or controversial content

Posting insensitive or controversial content can offend your followers and damage your brand reputation. Before posting anything, make sure it aligns with your brand values and is appropriate for your audience. If you wish to take a controversial stance on topics, be prepared to manage any comments you may receive.

Ignoring negative feedback

Ignoring negative feedback or responding defensively can make the situation worse and damage your reputation. If you make a mistake on social media, take responsibility and apologize if necessary.

Using automated messaging tools

Many automation tools are available to support social media management. Some are great at supporting productivity and time management, such as scheduling posts. However, you may come across automated messaging tools – not only are these unlikely to be permitted by the social media platform user terms and conditions, but in addition to breaching guidelines, they can also be viewed as inauthentic which would quickly impact your reputation and credibility. Take your time and create personalized messages when using social media.

Buying fake followers

While it may be tempting to buy followers to appear more popular, this practice can be harmful. Typically, the followers that are offered by third-party services are not real accounts and these followers will not engage with your content. Focus on building a genuine following through quality content.

Ignoring copyright and intellectual property ownership

When sharing content on social media, make sure you have the appropriate permissions to do so. Do not share content that belongs to someone else without giving credit or getting their permission first.

COMMON MISTAKES

✗ Not putting others first

Social media is not all about you. It is about your target audience – connecting with them through social media, and sharing content this is relevant and of interest to them.

✗ Expecting to go viral

While it's certainly possible to go viral on social media, this is often the exception rather than the rule. Focusing on trying to go viral will distract from building a strong, engaged following and sustainable results.

BUSINESS ESSENTIALS

✓ By making your content accessible, you are not only demonstrating your consideration for all individuals, but you will be able to increase your reach and engage with a wider audience. If you are unsure about your content, try using a contrast checker for images and a screen reader to read out your posts.

✓ Share social media dos and don'ts with your colleagues. Make them aware of the best practices and pitfalls that are involved with social media. Create guidelines for your own business and follow them.

BUSINESS ESSENTIALS

Overview of social media platforms

Facebook

Facebook's stated mission is to 'give people the power to build community and bring the world closer together'.

Facebook was first launched in 2004. It allows users to create a personal profile, connect with friends and family, and share updates, photos and videos. Businesses can set up Pages on social media. Users can follow a business to see content posted organically. Facebook has also developed a powerful advertising platform to allow businesses to promote products and services to highly targeted audiences. A key feature for businesses on Facebook is Groups. Businesses can set up Groups as a way to build a community around their products and services.

In 2021, the parent company of Facebook changed its name to Meta. The family of apps owned by the company includes Messenger, Instagram and WhatsApp.

www.facebook.com

Instagram

Instagram's mission is to 'capture and share the world's moments'. It was launched in 2010 and purchased by Facebook in 2012 for $1 billion. Instagram has evolved from its roots as a photo-sharing app to become a platform that is just as focused on video content. While photos are still a key part of the Instagram experience, the platform has increasingly emphasized video content in recent years.

www.instagram.com

LinkedIn

LinkedIn has a core focus on professional networking and career development. Launched in 2003, LinkedIn was acquired by Microsoft in 2016. Its vision is to 'create economic opportunity for every member of the global workforce.' Some of its key features include the ability to connect with other professionals, join groups related to specific industries or interests, and search for job opportunities. The platform also offers a range of tools for businesses and recruiters to find and hire talent, as well as to promote their products and services.

www.linkedin.com

Pinterest

Pinterest is a highly visual social media platform that allows users to curate content on a virtual pinboard. Some of its key features include the ability to save and organize pins, search for content by category or keyword, and follow other users or boards for inspiration. The platform also offers advertising and marketing options for businesses to reach a wider audience and promote their products or services. Pinterest has become an important tool for individuals and businesses alike to showcase their creativity and discover new ideas and trends.

www.pinterest.com

Snapchat

Snapchat empowers people to 'express themselves, live in the moment, learn about the world, and have fun together.' The multimedia app launched in 2011 and allows its users to send and receive photos and videos that disappear after they have been viewed. Snapchat has become one of the most popular social media platforms among younger generations.

Some of its key features include filters, lenses and stickers that can be applied to photos and videos.

www.snapchat.com

TikTok

One of the most downloaded apps over recent years, TikTok is the home of short-form video content. TikTok is known for its algorithm-driven 'For You' page that showcases content tailored to individual users' interests, and its editing tools that allow users to create and edit short videos with music, filters and other effects. The platform is also known for its popular trends, challenges and memes that often go viral across the Internet.

www.tiktok.com

X (formerly Twitter)

X is a platform known for sharing news, information and opinions. In the beginning, a Tweet was only 140 characters in length. Elon Musk purchased Twitter in October 2022 for $44 billion and has been making significant changes to the platform and its features. A key change is the launch of a subscription option now called X Premium (formerly Twitter Blue), which offers its subscribers additional features, including longer Tweets, an edit button, longer video uploads and also access to advertising.

www.twitter.com

Weibo

Weibo is a Chinese microblogging website that was launched in 2009 by Sina Corporation. Weibo allows users to share short messages, photos and videos with their followers, similar to X (formerly Twitter). The platform also offers features such as live streaming, online payments and a range of social networking functions.

www.weibo.com

YouTube

YouTube is a video-sharing platform that was launched in 2005 and purchased by Google in 2006. It allows users to upload, share and view videos on a wide range of topics, from music and entertainment to educational content and tutorials. Some of its key features include the ability to subscribe to channels, create playlists and comment on videos. Following the popularity of TikTok and Facebook and Instagram Reels, YouTube launched a short-form video format, called YouTube Shorts, in 2020.

www.youtube.com

Where to find more help

The Lighthouse

Staying on top of the ever-changing social media industry can be overwhelming and time-consuming. At www.thelighthouse.social, you will find a curated newsfeed with up-to-date news, directly from Facebook, X (formerly Twitter), LinkedIn, Instagram, TikTok, Pinterest, Snapchat, YouTube and various other trusted sources.

The Lighthouse also contains a library of valuable resources, including platform-specific tools, useful apps, books and training course recommendations as well as links to industry trend data reports.

Social Media Examiner

Social Media Examiner is an online magazine, blog and podcast sharing expert-led 'how-to' guides for various social media platforms. They also host an annual event, Social Media Marketing World. Visit www.socialmediaexaminer.com

Meta Blueprint

Official courses for Facebook and Instagram are available, directly from Meta, to help you learn how to use their family of apps. From getting started through to advertising campaigns, you can learn online for free. Certifications are also available.

Get started at: https://www.facebookblueprint.com/

LinkedIn Learning

LinkedIn Learning has a library of video courses taught by industry experts. You will find courses about how to use different social media platforms, marketing advice, guidance on content marketing, video marketing and more. LinkedIn Learning is available as part of a premium subscription.

Find a course at: www.linkedin.com/learning

TikTok Academy

TikTok also has a free online learning academy to guide businesses on how to get the most from the platform. You can enrol on courses at www.my .academywithtiktok.com/learn

Index